A GREAT EXPLORERS BOOK

Beyond the Sea of Ice

The Voyages of Henry Hudson

MIKAYA PRESS

NEW YORK

For Stu,
Who's launched me in a surprising new direction.

J.E.G.

✳

OTHER BOOKS BY JOAN ELIZABETH GOODMAN
A Long and Uncertain Journey: The 27,000 Mile Voyage of Vasco da Gama
Despite All Obstacles: La Salle and the Conquest of the Mississippi

Editor: Stuart Waldman
Design: Lesley Ehlers Design

Library of Congress Cataloging -in-publication Data

Goodman, Joan E.
Beyond the sea of ice : the voyages of Henry Hudson / by Joan
Elizabeth Goodman ; illustrated by Fernando Rangel ; with maps by
Bette Duke.
p.   cm. — (A great explorers books ; 1)
Summary: An account of Henry Hudson's four voyages in search of a
passage to the Orient in the early seventeenth century and the
discoveries made by him on the northeastern coast of America.
ISBN 0-9650493-8-8
1. Hudson, Henry, d. 1611 Juvenile literature.   2. Explorers—
America Biography Juvenile literature.   3. Explorers—England Biography
Juvenile literature.   4. America —Discovery and
exploration—English Juvenile literature [1. Hudson, Henry, d.
1611. 2. Explorers. 3. America—Discovery and exploration—
English.]   1. Rangel, Fernando, ill. 11 Duke, Bette.
111. Title.   1V. Series.
CURR   E129.H8G66 1999
910' .92—dc21
[B]   99-28782
                                                          CIP

10 9 8 7 6 5 4 3 2
Printed in China

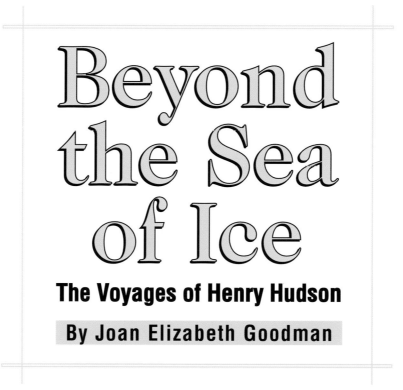

Beyond the Sea of Ice

The Voyages of Henry Hudson

By Joan Elizabeth Goodman

Illustrated by Fernando Rangel
With maps by Bette Duke

M I K A Y A P R E S S

NEW YORK

Half the crew of the *Discovery* was too ill to leave their berths. The other half was plotting mutiny and murder. All had suffered from frostbite, scurvy, hunger, and the long arctic winter of despair. The ship had been trapped in an icebound bay far in the north of America. Finally spring was melting the ice, setting the ship free. They could return to England, to home. But the captain talked of exploring the western reaches of this frigid sea, saying that it led to the long-sought passage to the Orient. The mutineers cared no more for his dreams of the East. They bound the captain, put him in a small boat with his son and the sick men, and cast them adrift. The *Discovery* sailed away from her captain, Henry Hudson, on June 22, 1611.

The beautiful river in New York, the great northern bay in Canada, and the strait leading to it bear his name. Though his name is well known, Henry Hudson himself remains a puzzle nearly four hundred years after his death. Not even a record of his birth exists. There is a lot of information about the four voyages he made from 1607 to 1611, but his career as explorer and navigator of the North Atlantic is filled with as many questions as answers.

Henry Hudson devoted his life to exploring and charting the northern seas, hoping to find the elusive passage to the Orient. Until the 1400s most of the world beyond Europe was as remote and mysterious as the far reaches of the galaxy are for modern people. Then came the period known as the Renaissance. It was a time when great changes were taking place in the arts, in literature, and in science. Europeans began to look at the world around them and wonder. They studied the placement and movement of heavenly bodies. They investigated nature. They began to explore the vast unknown seas that surrounded the known earth and to record what they found in maps.

The great age of exploration was sparked by one large event, the

Turkish conquest of Constantinople in 1453. This shut down the overland trade route from the Far East to Europe that had been used for centuries. But Europe had grown accustomed to the spices brought from the Spice Islands in the Indian Ocean. Meats were heavily spiced to mask their often rancid nature. Even sweet dishes such as pies and puddings were strongly flavored with cinnamon, cardamom, and clove. Spices were costly, but Europeans of the Middle Ages and Renaissance craved them. Food without spice was inedible. Europe also needed the precious metals and gems of the East. Before paper money, these resources were used as currency. And Europeans who could afford it demanded the silks of China. Another way had to be found to the Orient.

In the Renaissance the science of the earth's geography was based on theories of ancient Greek philosophers, popular beliefs, and misinformation. No one knew exactly how big the earth was, nor what it looked like. But there were many theories. It was commonly thought that the earth was divided into balanced masses of land and that all the world's seas were connected and in constant flow. The earth was thought to be much smaller

First Voyage

In 1607, the Muscovy Company chose Henry Hudson to lead a new voyage of discovery. The Hudson family had a long association with the company. Hudson's grandfather was one of its founders. Uncles and cousins were company agents or sailors. There was a Christopher Hudson trading in Russia, and a Thomas Hudson, captain of a company ship.

Young boys were sent by the company to far-flung outposts where they studied foreign languages and the intricacies of trade. Some boys went to sea. They grew up on the merchant ships, learning the arts of navigation and sailing. Most likely Henry Hudson was one of these boys, born into and raised by the Muscovy Company. His early life is unknown, but we can be sure that the shrewd merchants of the Muscovy Company wouldn't have hired him unless they knew he was experienced and able to succeed.

On April 19, Hudson knelt at St. Ethleburge's Church in London, with his son John and the other ten members of the crew, to ask the Lord's blessing and protection. They would need it. They were about to embark on a journey across the top of the world. Their ship, the *Hopewell*, was a small, comfortless wooden boat. The charts to guide them were based on rumor and hope as much as fact. In 1607, measuring latitude depended on instruments that were extremely difficult to use on a wave-tossed ship even in good weather and impossible to use in storms. There was no way at all to calculate longitude. A captain could never know exactly where he was.

than it actually is, and China to be much closer to Europe. It was also believed that the ancient Greeks had reached China by sailing along the north coast of Russia.

A group of wealthy English merchants banded together to find this northeastern passage. They called themselves the Merchant Adventurers. In May of 1553, they sent three ships north around Norway and Finland through seas of storm and ice. Only one of the ships and crew survived. They made it to the northern coast of Russia and proceeded overland to Moscow.

The Merchant Adventurers secured trading rights and became known as the Muscovy Company. The Russian trade was profitable, but the frigid winters limited the access of ships, making it extremely difficult. Beyond Russia were the Spice Islands and the markets of China and India. That was the real treasure trove. The Muscovy Company renewed its efforts to find a northern route to the Orient.

1607-1611

The Four Voyages of Henry Hudson

Keep the other side of this
page open. You can read about
Henry Hudson's travels and
follow them on the map at
the same time.

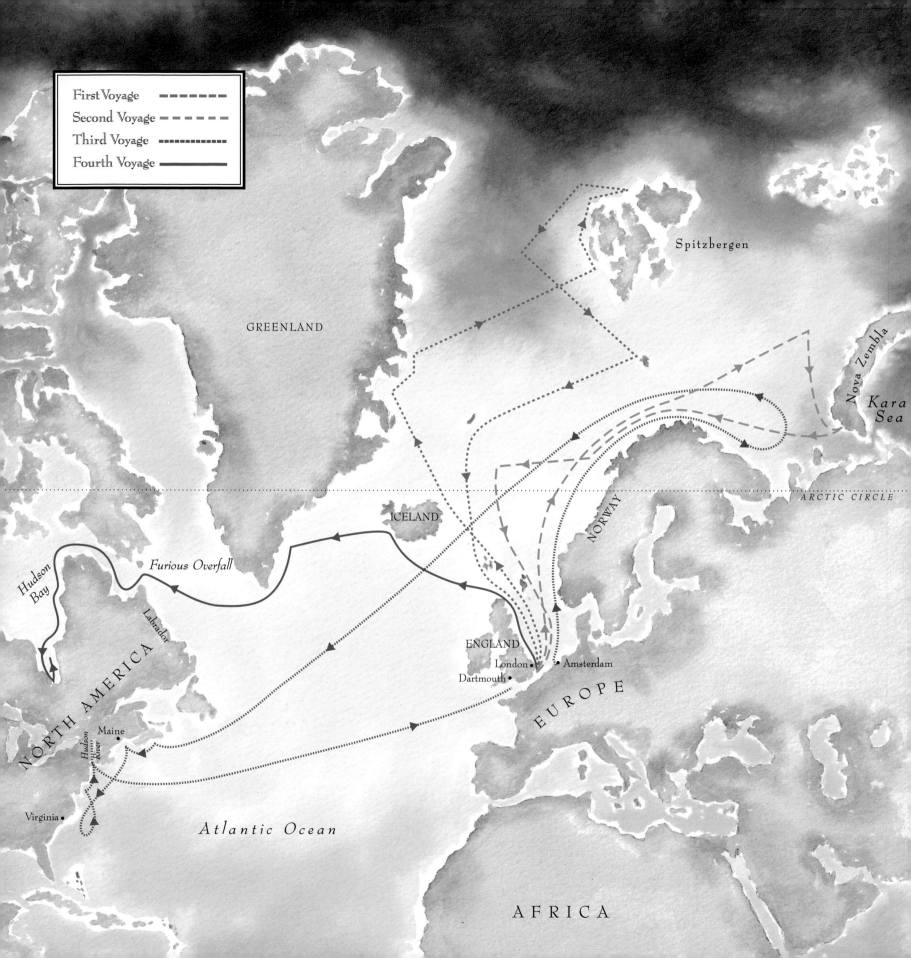

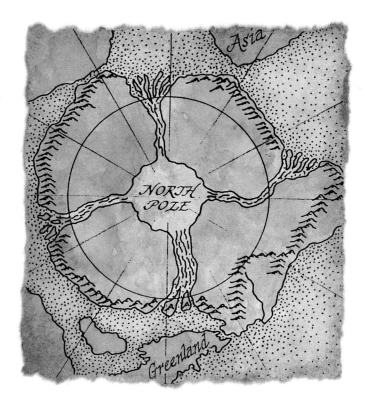

It was a wonder that anyone set foot aboard ship, let alone embarked on a voyage of discovery, when only half of the ships going out ever returned. Sailing into the ice-choked northern seas might prove to be the most dangerous expedition of all.

Hudson's orders were to find a route straight across the North Pole. It was known that the summer sun shone directly on the North Pole for twenty-four hours a day. Geographers reasoned that this constant, intense sunlight melted the polar cap, creating a warm, navigable sea. If Henry Hudson could find a passage through the encircling ice to that sea, he would be the first to claim a route to the Orient for the Muscovy Company and for England.

On May 1, they set sail. The *Hopewell* headed to Greenland and then sailed northeast. They were often sailing in an icy fog. Yet they continued going in spite of the miserable conditions aboard ship. The only source of warmth was the cook's small fire. The ropes were crusted with ice, cutting into the men's hands as they tried to set the frozen sails. When the men got wet, they stayed wet. And their wet woolen clothes froze as well.

16th-century maps depicted an open polar sea from Greenland to Asia.

Through the end of June, the *Hopewell* pursued the northern passage. Henry Hudson was looking for something that didn't exist. It was as if he were blind, trying to find an opening in a solid wall. He kept feeling his way, sure that the opening was just ahead, but all he found was wall — a wall of ice.

On June 27, the *Hopewell* came to Spitzbergen, a group of islands extending far north of the Arctic Circle. They saw seals and walruses. Whales swam in the frigid waters, dwarfing the small ship. The seas varied in color from blue to deep green to pitch black. At the northern tip of Spitzbergen, this small wooden vessel, with a crew of twelve, was within 577 miles of the North Pole. The *Hopewell* had sailed farther north than any ship had ever gone before.

And there they stopped. There was no hope of a passage through the ice surrounding them. There was no northern route over the Pole. Hudson gave the command to return to England on July 31.

Yet, instead of following the most direct route home, the *Hopewell* went west toward North America. Why?

There were many theories about where a passage to the Orient could be found. Many believed there was a passage in the far north of America. Since the polar route was blocked, Henry Hudson would go this way. He was willing to continue searching until he found China.

The *Hopewell* headed four hundred miles west and then abruptly changed course, returning to England. No one knows exactly what happened. Perhaps the ship ran into bad weather. Perhaps supplies were low. Perhaps the crew had had enough of fogbound, frozen seas. Whatever the reason, the voyage that had begun so full of hope and expectation was over.

The Journal of Henry Hudson
The Hopewell, 1607

June 25
Tonight we saw flocks of birds with black backs, white bellies and long, sharp-pointed tails. We supposed that land was not far off, but we could not see it, the fog being so close....

July 1
We headed northeast for the shore hoping to find an open sea. About noon we were surrounded by ice.

July 4
It was very cold and our shrouds and sails were frozen.

July 12
Then we saw ice ahead of us....The combination of thick fog, calm wind and a sea with ice drifting towards us brought us close to danger. It pleased God at the very instant to give us a small gale, which was our deliverance; to Him therefore we give praise.

Second Voyage

The *Hopewell*'s failure to reach the Orient didn't discourage the Muscovy Company, nor Henry Hudson. Three months after his return to England, he signed on to command the *Hopewell* on a voyage eastward along the northern coast of Russia. This northeast passage was the same route attempted by the original Merchant Adventurers some fifty years before.

A northeast passage remained a very popular theory. We now know the impossibility of this plan. The Russian coastline extends much further east and north than what was shown on the best

The solid line on this map is the northern Russian coastline that Henry Hudson hoped to find. The dotted line shows the actual Russian coast.

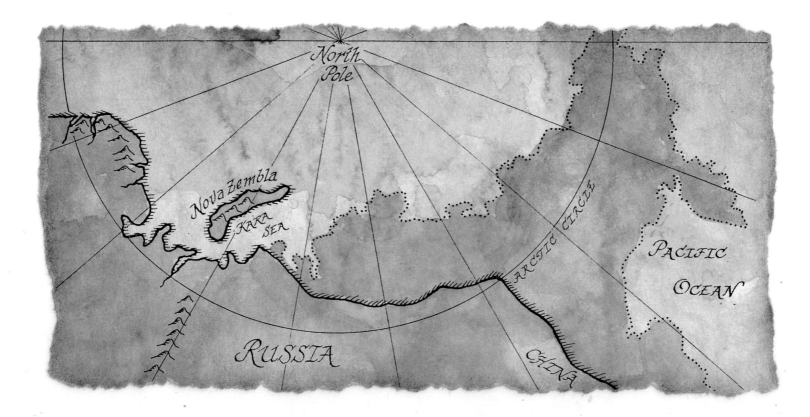

**The Journal of Henry Hudson
The Hopewell, 1608**

June 15

She was close to the ship's side and looking earnestly at the men....Her back and breasts were like a woman's, her body as big as ours, her skin very white, and she had long black hair hanging down behind. When she dove they saw her tail which was like the tail of a porpoise, and speckled like a mackerel.

maps in Henry Hudson's day. The north coast of Russia is one of the most inhospitable places on earth. But geographers of the early seventeenth century believed otherwise.

Heading north, the *Hopewell* again found fog and "searching cold." By June 7, they'd rounded the northernmost point of Norway. Soon after, they encountered ice and storm-blown, angry seas. On the morning of June 15, they came upon something rarer—a mermaid.

Two seamen described her in detail. It was an age newly awakened to science and learning, but people still believed in mermaids and monsters. Hudson recorded the mermaid sighting in his log as matter-of-factly as he noted the weather.

Hudson planned to head northeast around Nova Zembla, a long, crescent-shaped island to the north of Russia. He believed that the Kara Sea, which lay on the other side of Nova Zembla, led to the Orient. He tried to go around the north of the island but the ice forced him to retreat. He didn't go around the southern tip because earlier explorers had found that route nearly impossible to navigate. He had one last hope. His charts showed a strait that cut across Nova Zembla. If Hudson could find that strait, might he not also find the open sea and the easy passage to China on the other side?

Dangers arose even in the calmest weather. There was constant fog and ice to contend with. On June 30, at the mouth of a river, great slabs of ice propelled by a strong current swept past the ship, threatening to crush her.

The men fought the ice as best they could, pushing it away from the ship with oars and spars. As dangerous as it was, Henry Hudson felt this river might lead them to the strait they were looking for. Following the river to a bay, he sent a small boat to investigate another large river to the north. The men reported that it was broad, deep, and salty as the sea. This raised his hopes even further. A river of salt water indicated a strait. He was sure that this would lead to the Orient. But it wasn't a strait, and it flowed into a landlocked, ice-filled bay.

Hudson's hopes of finding a northeast passage were over.

Unable to fulfill his orders, he was free to return home. Instead, on July 27, he headed the *Hopewell* west, just as he had on the first voyage.

Despite the nearly two months of hardship already endured, Hudson wanted to go on. He was willing to sail thousands of miles across the Atlantic to put the theories of a passage in the north of America to the test.

But the Atlantic crossing didn't go well from the beginning. The winds were against Henry Hudson. More important, the crew was, too. The captain's commitment to finding a passage to the Orient was not theirs. Normally a captain's wishes were law. But a captain had to be able to enforce that law. Hudson did not or could not. As much as he wished to continue west, after only eleven days, he headed the *Hopewell* for home. Hudson's ambition wasn't enough. He had to have a willing, or at least obedient, crew.

Third Voyage

After two failures the Muscovy Company refused to sponsor another voyage of discovery. Perhaps the merchants had lost confidence in finding a northern passage, but Henry Hudson had not. If he could not convince the English merchants that a northern route to the Orient existed, and that he was the man to find it, then he would go elsewhere.

In the fall of 1608, Hudson went to Amsterdam and began negotiating with the merchants of the Dutch East India Company. The Dutch tried to put him off for another year. He could not wait. He began talking with the French ambassador. The Dutch were England's rivals, while the French were outright enemies, but Hudson was willing to sail for either of them. He was determined to go where others had turned back. He would find a route to the Orient, and he would do it for anyone who would give him a ship. When the Dutch merchants got wind of his dealings with the French, they hurriedly signed him on.

On January 8, 1609, Hudson was named master of the *Halve Maen* (*Half Moon*). He signed a contract to search for a northeast passage "by the north around the north side of Nova Zembla." Although this was exactly what he'd already attempted and abandoned as hopeless, the Dutch believed it was possible. Shortly before sailing, the Dutch revised the contract to read that Hudson was not to "think" of discovering any route other than that around Nova Zembla. He was to succeed at finding the northeast passage. If not, he was to return immediately to Holland. The Dutch merchants must have suspected that Hudson had another route in mind. They were right.

While in Amsterdam, Henry Hudson met with Peter Plancius, perhaps the greatest geographer of the age. The two men discussed possible northern routes. Hudson traced out a map of the north coast of America, showing where he hoped to find a northwest passage. That was where his ambition lay, no matter what his orders said.

The English sailors who had been on the *Hopewell* were prepared for the ice and fog that engulfed them as they rounded the coast of Norway. The Dutch crew, used to sailing in the warm south seas, were not. They had been complaining since they passed north of England. Finally the men confronted Captain Hudson in his cabin. The crew refused to go any farther.

This was mutiny.

Hudson remained calm. Although it was the gravest crime at sea for a crew to turn upon its master, he didn't threaten the men with hanging. Instead, he bargained with them. He brought out a letter from his friend, Captain John Smith, indicating a strait north of the Virginia Colony, in America, that led to China.

He gave his crew a choice. They could look for a passage in the far north of America. Or they could follow the advice of John Smith and go south to Virginia. The crew chose to look for John Smith's passage, which would at least be warm. Hudson cared only that they went west. Once there, he was determined to explore both possibilities.

In many maps of the time, a large segment of America was shown as a narrow strip separating the Atlantic and Pacific Oceans. Finding a passage north of Virginia seemed reasonable.

Surviving rough weather and one storm so fierce it broke a mast, the *Half Moon* came to Maine on July 17. She anchored in Penobscot Bay, where a new mast was cut.

Here, for the first time, Henry Hudson and his men encountered the people of America. The crew of the *Half Moon* had never met anyone like them, but they were already prejudiced against these "Indians," as the Europeans called them. Earlier explorers had returned with exaggerated tales of the savages found in the New World. A picture in one of the first atlases of the world showed Europe as a ruling queen and America as a naked cannibal.

The Penobscots were vastly different from the crew of the *Half Moon*. Their dress, their language, their customs were incomprehensible to Hudson and his men. As friendly as the Indians might seem, the crew regarded them with distrust and suspicion. One of the English sailors, Robert Juet, often described Indians as "Savages" in his journal.

And yet the men of the *Half Moon* came prepared to trade. Henry Hudson had brought red cloth, knives, hatchets, and beads to exchange for silken beaver skins and fine, thick furs of fox and marten. The high-quality North American furs were already in great demand in Europe. Savages or not, here was profit.

Just before the *Half Moon* left the Maine coast, Robert Juet led twelve men ashore, armed with muskets. They drove the Indians from their homes and robbed them. Juet wrote, "…as they would have done to us."

Why did Henry Hudson allow his men to assault the Indians who had traded peaceably with them? Did he share his men's attitude toward the natives, or were the men beyond his control? One thing is certain: the Europeans were so sure of their own superiority, and the rightness of their actions, that what would have been criminal in Europe was somehow justified in America.

The *Half Moon* quickly sailed away from her treachery, south to Cape Hatteras, opposite the Virginia Colony. Then she turned north, hugging the shore, looking for the strait Smith had promised.

On September 5, the log entry read: "Two days ago we came upon three great rivers, and today have found a very good harbor."

This simple statement marked the beginning of Hudson's most famous exploration—New York harbor and the river that now bears his name.

Not even the skyscraper forest of modern New York City can dwarf the majestic river. Imagine what it was like for Hudson to sail past Manhattan Island's fragrant meadows, hills covered with oak and birch and hemlock, and the sheer cliffs of New Jersey's Palisades. Europe had forests and rivers, but nothing to compare with this wild and beautiful place. Hudson wrote, "It is as pleasant a land as one need tread upon." Then he described its timber, copper, and iron, since that was what the practical Dutch merchants cared about.

Trading began almost immediately. Indians of the Lenape tribe came aboard to exchange green tobacco for beads and knives. A party from the *Half Moon* went ashore. They saw many men, women, and children. Some were dressed in skins of deer and foxes, and some in shimmering cloaks of feathers. Copper necklaces and arm bands gleamed against their dark skin.

**The Journal of Henry Hudson
The Half Moon, 1609**

September 4
Their food is maize or Indian corn which they cook by baking and it is exellent eating. They all came round the ship, one after another, in their canoes, which are made of a single hollowed tree; their weapons are bows and arrows, pointed with sharp stones, which they fasten with hard resin. They had no houses but slept under the blue heavens.

Manhattan Island

On September 6, John Colman and four other men took the small boat and went exploring. They passed grassy meadows and stands of fine, tall trees. The breeze carried the sweet scent of flowers. Suddenly, two canoes filled with Lenape warriors came at them. The men took to their oars, rowing hard for the ship.

The canoes closed in on them. Colman was about to fire his musket when an arrow pierced his throat. He slumped over his oar, dead. The men fired many shots, and the Lenape retreated.

Night came on and with it a pouring rain. The lamp sputtered and died. In the dark and rain the men couldn't find the ship. They rowed back and forth all night, sure that the Indians would return and kill them all. The dead man lay at their feet, washed clean by the rain.

Was Colman's death the result of a random act of violence, or was it in some way provoked by the crew? Most likely it was a response to earlier encounters with Europeans. Some coastal Indians had bitter experiences with these strangely dressed, hairy men from across the sea. Giovanni da Verrazano had tried taking Indian captives when he came to New York harbor in 1524. Éstevan Gómez, who came soon after Verrazano, actually captured a number of Indians. It was said that Gómez had a cargo of *clavos* (cloves) from the Spice Islands. In fact, he carried *esclavos* (slaves) from America.

Perhaps in reaction to Colman's death, Henry Hudson took two Indians prisoner.

The *Half Moon* then proceeded upriver. Did Hudson believe that the wide flow of silver water was the northwest passage? Neither his journal nor Juet's ever described it as anything other than a river. Hudson didn't deceive himself that this was the route to the Orient. Yet he followed it as far north as he could.

On September 15, near what is now West Point, the prisoners escaped.

Farther upriver, within sight of the Catskill Mountains, relations with the natives improved. Henry Hudson went ashore as the guest of a Mahican chief. Unlike the Lenape, the inland Mahicans had little or no experience with Europeans. Hudson may have been their first visitor from the Old World. The Mahicans were very hospitable. Hudson and his men were brought to a round house built of oak bark. Mats were spread on the ground, and food was brought in red wooden bowls. Two hunters were sent for game, and a fat dog was skinned and roasted.

When Hudson was about to leave, the Mahicans protested. Wanting him to remain, and to show he had nothing to fear from their weapons, they broke their arrows and cast them on the fire.

**The Journal of Henry Hudson
The Half Moon, 1609**

September 18
I sailed to the shore in one of their canoes with an old man, who was the chief of the tribe consisting of 40 men and 17 women; these I saw in a well constructed house of oak bark and circular in shape. . . .

The land is the finest for cultivation that I ever in my life set foot upon, and it also abounds in trees of every description. The natives are a very good people.

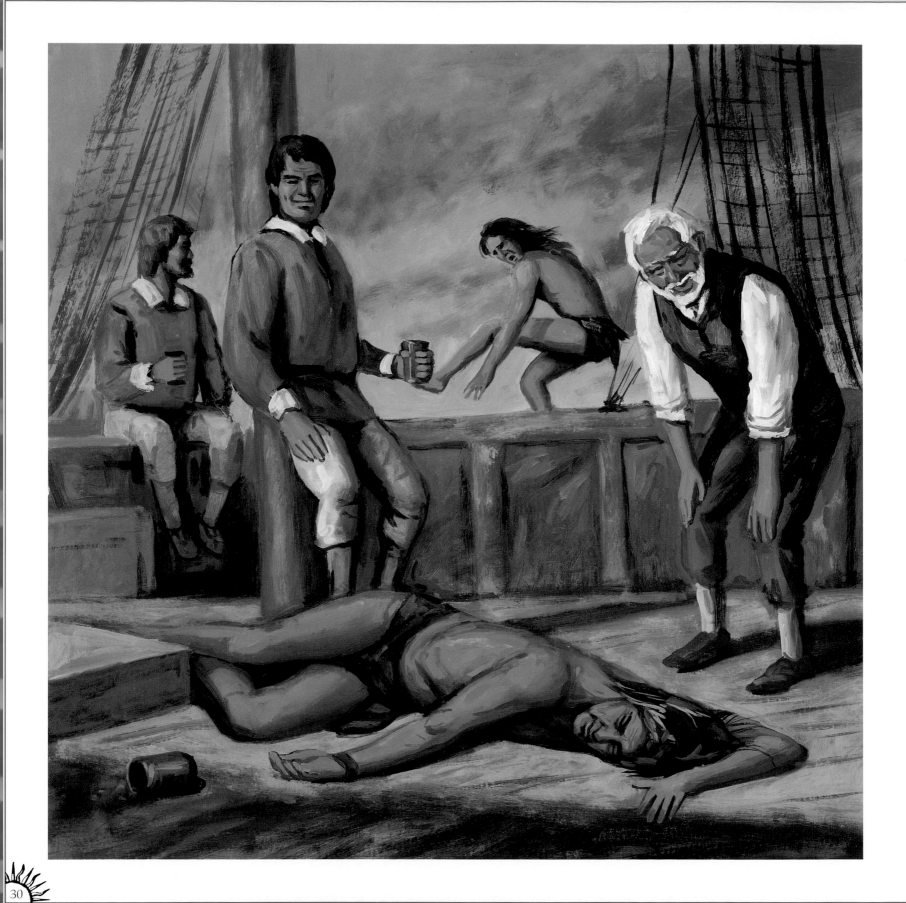

Throughout the voyage upriver, the Indians continued to welcome and trade with the men of the *Half Moon*. At one village, the chief gave Hudson strings of wampum. He made a long speech, opening wide his arms. He seemed to offer Hudson the vast country all around them.

Despite these friendly encounters, the crew's attitude toward the natives remained mistrustful. Hudson decided to put the Mahican leaders to a strange test. The Indians were invited aboard the *Half Moon* and given wine and strong drink. The plan was to make them drunk and see if they would reveal treachery. Not having any experience with alcohol, one of the Indians fell into a stupor. His terrified companions hurried off the boat.

Returning the next day, they found the man completely recovered. Venison, tobacco, and wampum were brought to Hudson, gifts to appease him and protect them from the captain's magic drink.

Somewhere near what is now Albany, the river became too shallow for the *Half Moon* to continue. She changed course, heading back downriver, and into even greater difficulty. Twice the ship was grounded on mud banks. Trouble began when they again encountered coastal Indians.

On October 1, an exchange of goods turned ugly when an Indian climbed into the officers' cabin and stole a pillow, two shirts, and two bandoliers. The mate shot and killed him. The rest fled. But one Indian, who was in the water, clung to the *Half Moon*. The cook cut off his hand and he drowned. More bloodshed followed as the *Half Moon* neared the northern end of Manhattan. One of the two Lenapes taken captive on the voyage upriver led a war party intent on revenge. They attacked the ship, but bows and arrows were no match against muskets and cannons. Several Indians died. On October 4, the *Half Moon* sailed out of New York harbor, her hold full of precious furs, a trail of blood in her wake.

**The Journal of Robert Juet
The Half Moon, 1609**

October 2
I shot a light cannon and killed two. The rest fled into the woods. They sent off another canoe manned by nine or ten. I sent off another shot from the cannon and killed one of them. Then our men with their muskets killed three or four more. They went their way and we got down six miles, where we anchored in a bay on the other side of the river and clear of all danger from them. Here was a very good piece of ground.... It is on the side of the river called Manna-hata.

Henry Hudson headed for Europe. The Dutch mate suggested wintering in North America so they could continue searching for the northwest passage in the spring. This might have appealed to Henry Hudson, but he knew that the *Half Moon* didn't have enough provisions to see them through a long winter and further exploration. And he wouldn't have put his mutinous crew to that test.

No doubt he knew that his crew wasn't so much interested in finding the northwest passage as they were in delaying their return to Holland. They had reason to worry about their reception in Amsterdam; the Dutch merchants could hang them all for mutiny. Perhaps Hudson wasn't eager to face his Dutch employers, either. Not only had he gone directly against explicit sailing orders, he hadn't found the passage to the Orient. On November 7, 1609, the *Half Moon* landed in Dartmouth, England.

Hudson wrote to the Dutch East India Company requesting payment for services and a re-outfitting of the *Half Moon*. He proposed an early spring voyage to find the northwest passage. Before the Dutch could answer him, the English authorities stepped in. Hudson was commanded not to leave England, nor to serve any country but England.

It was well begun. Some of England's most powerful and wealthy men, including Prince Henry, supported the voyage. Henry Hudson would finally be able to look for the passage to the Orient where he had always believed it to be—in the far northwest.

The seventeenth of April 1610, Hudson set out from London aboard the *Discovery* with a crew of twenty-three. Five of the men had sailed with him before, including his son and Robert Juet as mate. It is a great puzzle why Hudson chose Juet. He'd had plenty of experience with this difficult man. Juet had been aboard the *Hopewell* and the *Half Moon*. He may well have been involved in mutiny, and he'd led the attack on the Penobscots. But Robert Juet was an excellent navigator, better than Hudson himself. There weren't many men with Juet's ability, and fewer still who were willing to sign on for a voyage of discovery. Hudson must have been willing to risk all of Juet's known faults because he felt that this man would be the one to plot their course to the Orient. And that was more important to him than anything else.

Trouble soon started. On May 11, the *Discovery* came to Iceland, where bad weather and contrary winds delayed her. Storms were also brewing amongst the crew. Henry Greene, a known troublemaker, picked a fight with another seaman. Hudson sided with Greene, causing much ill feeling. Robert Juet began talking mutiny within sight of Iceland. On June 1, nearing Greenland, Juet threatened to turn the ship around. Hudson made peace with Juet and the voyage continued, but the damage was done. Juet had poisoned the minds of the crew. And Captain Hudson had shown himself to be a weak leader.

The Journal of
Abacuk Prickett
The Discovery, 1610

July
We had a storm that brought the ice upon us so fast that finally we were forced to attach ourselves to the largest piece of ice and let the ship lie there. Today some of the men fell sick, I will not say it is on account of fear, but I did see some signs of trouble.

Greenland was sighted on June 4. The *Discovery* navigated through icy seas around its southern tip, then north and west toward Labrador. By June 25, they'd come to a strait whose entrance was known as the Furious Overfall because of its violent outpouring of water. It had been discovered in 1587 by John Davis, who was sure that this northern strait eventually led to an ocean beyond. Hudson agreed and saw the riches of the Orient within reach. Instead, what lay ahead was a monthlong nightmare of storms, fog, giant icebergs, murderous ice floes, and most dangerous of all—his mutinous crew.

What started with grumbling soon became a confrontation. Robert Juet mocked Hudson's claim that they'd be in India by February. Hudson got out his charts and showed the men that they'd already gone farther than any Englishman before them. Normally, a captain never showed his charts and never explained himself to his crew. A captain gave orders and his crew obeyed. Henry Hudson didn't have that control. Yet, somehow, he convinced the men to keep going.

Maps like this one convinced Henry Hudson that, once past the Furious Overfall, an open sea would flow into the Strait of Anian. This was a mythical body of water that geographers believed led to China.

In early August, the *Discovery* sailed through a narrow pass. On either side were stark, soaring cliffs of rock and ice. Yet this grim corridor opened to a clear, ice-free sea. It was Hudson's first view of what must have seemed to him the end of his troubles. He was sure this would take him to the Anian Strait, the fabled passage to the Orient.

Instead, it led to an enormous bay. Hudson spent the next three months looking for the Anian. He had nothing to guide him but his belief that it existed and that it was only a matter of time until they found it.

The complaining began again, with Juet the leader of the dissent. Another captain might have put him in irons. Henry Hudson held a trial. Juet was demoted and his pay cut. It didn't solve the problem. In fact, it made it worse.

By the end of October it was already too late to get out the way they'd come. Ice had trapped them in the southern corner of the bay. On November 1 the *Discovery* dropped anchor in a pocket sheltered by three hills. Abacuk Prickett and Philip Staffe, the ship's carpenter, were sent ashore to find a sheltered place to spend the winter.

There was no good place—only marsh and muck and stunted trees, twisted ugly by the wind. They chose the least bad place. And working like donkeys, they hauled the ship on shore. By November 10, the *Discovery* was frozen fast.

In December, Hudson ordered Philip Staffe to build them a house. The carpenter argued that it was too late in the year. The wood was hard as stone, and the nails would freeze in his hands. Hudson swore at his carpenter, threatening to hang him if he didn't obey. Staffe pieced together a shack, but it was of little use against the brutal winds and piercing cold.

The arctic winter closed around them. The men suffered from the unbearable cold. The lack of fresh fruits and vegetables brought on scurvy. This disease caused their gums to turn black and bleed. Teeth fell out, and some men grew too weak to move. The days of endless night dragged on.

The birds saved them. First it was the snow-white arctic ptarmigans. They came in flocks all the long winter. Hudson reckoned they'd killed some twelve hundred of them. When the ptarmigans left in early spring, other fowl came—ducks, geese, and teal.

The Journal of Abacuk Prickett
The Discovery, 1610

December

The carpenter told him that the snow and frost were such that he neither could nor would do it. And when the master heard this he called for him in his cabin to strike him, calling him many foul names and threatening to hang him. The carpenter told our master that he knew his job better than the master and that he was no house carpenter. The house was finally made, with much labor, but of little use.

The Journal of Abacuk Prickett
The Discovery, 1611

June

He brought all the bread out of the bread room, which came to a pound for each man's share. He gave them also a receipt, insisting that they have it to show if it please God that they came home. And he wept when he gave it to them.

By late spring the birds were gone. The men had little luck fishing. They scavenged along the shores, eating frogs and moss, which Abacuk Prickett said was like eating a rotten fence post. The ship's stores of food were nearly gone.

In May, as the days grew warmer and the ice began to break up, they had their first encounter with an Inuit native. Hudson gave him trinkets. The man went away and came back with deer and beaver skins. When Hudson haggled with him over the price, the man went away and never returned.

Seven of the crew were sent in the shallop, the ship's small boat, and netted 500 fine fish. But that was the most they ever got, and many days yielded only a few. Hunger grew, and so did fear.

Hudson took the shallop, hoping to find natives and trade with them for food. It was a dangerous moment to leave his crew on their own. All the while he was gone, the men talked and the plotting began. The crew feared that Hudson wouldn't give up the search for the northwest passage and that they would die looking for it.

Hudson returned to the ship after several days, empty handed. He divided up the remaining bread and cheese so that each man would get some of the good and some of the rotten. It didn't amount to more than a couple of pounds per man. The men accused him of holding back.

On the eighteenth of June, when the men were at their

lowest, Henry Hudson ordered that the men's sea chests be broken open to find what food they might be hoarding. A sea chest was the only private place a sailor had. It was wrong, even for a captain, to invade it. It was the final straw.

Three days later the men acted.

As Hudson left his cabin, still in his night clothes, he was seized and bound. He was put into the shallop with his son and seven others—men who were too sick to fight. The mutineers planned to spare Philip Staffe, as they might need the carpenter's skills to get home. Staffe would have none of it. He chose to go with Hudson. He asked for his sea chest, gun, and an iron pot with some grain. These things were lowered into the shallop with Staffe.

The mutineers sailed out of the ice with the shallop in tow. Soon it was cut loose, and all the sails of the *Discovery* were set. She ran before the wind as if fleeing an enemy. Through it all, Henry Hudson said nothing. He met his certain death with calm dignity.

Neither Greene or Juet survived the *Discovery's* homeward journey. Greene and three others were killed by natives soon after the mutiny. The food ran out and the men ate candle wax and bird bones. Juet "...died miserably for mere want."

At their trial, the eight who survived blamed Juet and Greene for the mutiny and Henry Hudson for being a failed commander. The court believed them and they were acquitted, but the truth can never be known.

The Journal of Abacuk Prickett The Discovery, 1611

June 22

Now, all the poor men were in the shallop, their names as follows:

Henry Hudson, John Hudson, Arnold Lodlo, Sidrack Faner, Philip Staffe, Thomas Wydhouse, Adam Moore, Henry King and Michael Bute.

The ship sailed out of the ice with the shallop tied to its stern, and when it was well out, they cut the shallop adrift. They set the ship's topsails and sailed eastward into a clear sea.

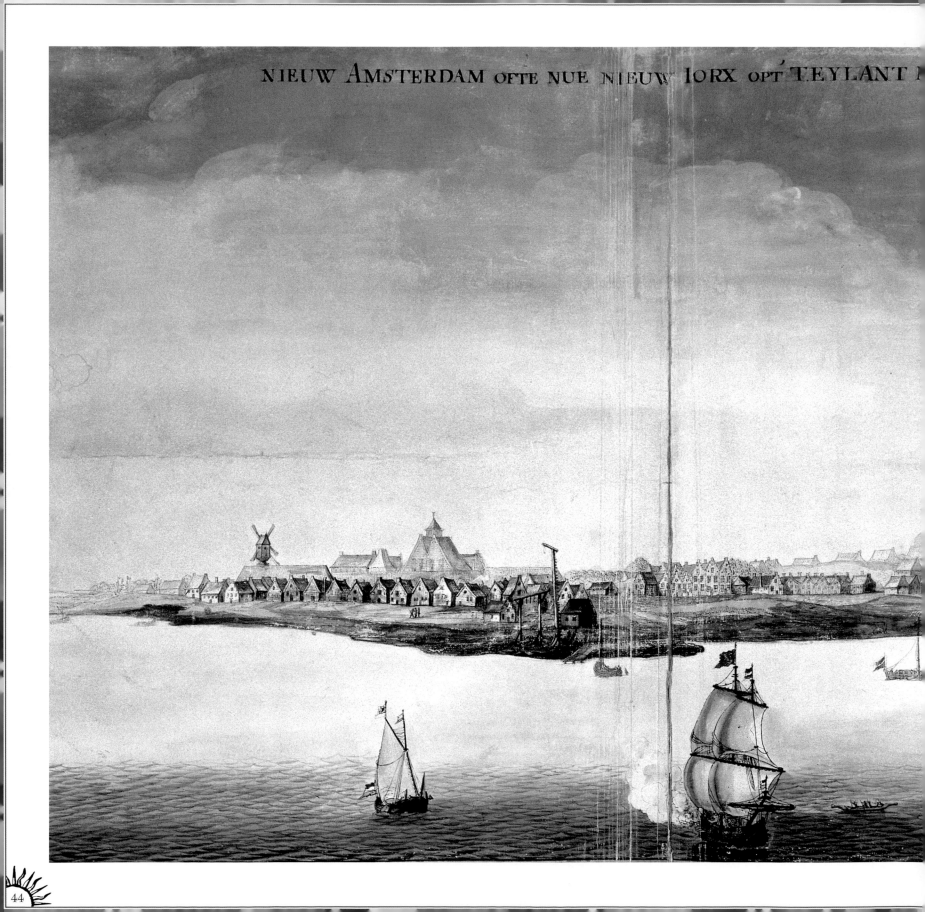

NIEUW AMSTERDAM OFTE NUE NIEUW IORX OPT' T. EYLANT M

The belief in the northwest passage was still very much alive. The *Discovery* was sent five more times to find it, but never did. The idea of the northwest passage persisted through the nineteenth century. In 1906, after three years of icebound questing, Roald Amundsen did find a western route through North America. He commanded a steam-driven, iron-hulled ship that was quite different from Hudson's frail, wooden vessel.

The remains of Henry Hudson were never found. Fur trappers for the Hudson Bay Company reported finding the ruins of a house thought to have been built by Staffe. There were some tales told by the natives of Labrador of a small band of white men found in the icy regions who married into the tribe.

In his story "Rip Van Winkle," Washington Irving named Henry Hudson as one of the ghosts haunting the Catskill Mountains, keeping "...a kind of vigil there every twenty years, with his crew of the *Half Moon*; being permitted in this way to revisit the scenes of his enterprise, and keep a guardian eye upon the river..." ⚓

In this painting, done only forty years after Henry Hudson first sailed past its shores, New Amsterdam (now New York City) was already a well-established community.

AUTHOR'S NOTE

While researching this book I was able to visit the replica of the Half Moon *docked in Kingston, New York. Setting foot on that ship was a revelation. It was so small. Even with only eighteen men, it would have been terribly crowded and miserably uncomfortable. The crew slept in a dank crawl space. The captain's cabin was a little more comfortable, but far from luxurious. It was amazing that anyone would set sail on the Half Moon under the safest conditions. Yet the desire to find a new route to the East was so strong that men set aside comfort and safety in its pursuit.*

Throughout the text I've used the term "Indian" to refer to the people of North America because that is the word Henry Hudson used, even though, by 1600, Europeans understood that the land across the Atlantic was not India. I've also used Nova Zembla to define the crescent north of Russia, although, on modern maps, it's known as Novaya Zemlya.

The journal entries from each voyage have been modernized in regard to spelling and somewhat revised for clarity.

First Voyage

The Hopewell—1607

Henry Hudson, *Master*
William Collin, *mate*
Thomas Baxter
John Colman
John Cooke
James Beubery
James Skrutton
John Pleyce
Richard Day
James Knight
James Young
John Hudson *(Henry's Son)*

Second Voyage

The Hopewell—1608

Henry Hudson, *Master*
Robert Juet, *Mate*
Ludlow Arnall
John Cooke
Humfrey Gilby
John Braunch
John Adrey
James Strutton
Michael Feirce
Thomas Hills
Philip Stacie
John Barnes
Richard Tomson
Robert Raynor
John Hudson

Third Voyage

The Half Moon—1609

Although the ship carried 16 to 18 men,
only the names of three are known.
Henry Hudson, *Master*
Robert Juet
John Colman

Fourth Voyage

The Discovery—1610-1611

Cast adrift in the shallop

Henry Hudson, *Master*
John Hudson
Michael Bute
Philip Staffe
Thomas Wydhouse
Adam Moore
Arnold Lodlo
Sidrack Faner
Henry King

Died during the voyage or return

Robert Juet, *Mate*
John Williams
William Wilson
John Thomas
Michael Pierce
Adrian Motter
Henry Greene

Returned to England

Robert Bylot
Edward Wilson
Francis Clements
Silvanus Bond
Abacuk Prickett
Bennet Mathew
Nicholas Syms
Adrian Motte

CREDITS

Bette Duke: *pp. 9, 11, 14, 20, 35*

Museum of the City of New York, The J. Clarence Davis Collection: *pp. 44-45*

Fernando Rangel: *pp. 13, 17, 18, 21, 22, 25, 26, 29, 30, 36, 39, 40, 43,*